T0130273

Soul Expression

Highgate Park London

By
Magi Traynor

Balboa Press books may be ordered through booksellers or by contacting:

Balboa Press
A Division of Hay House
1663 Liberty Drive
Bloomington, IN 47403
www.balboapress.com
1 (877) 407-4847

ISBN: 978-1-9822-2522-3 (sc)
ISBN: 978-1-9822-2523-0 (e)

Print information available on the last page.

Balboa Press rev. date: 04/12/2019

BALBOA
PRESS
A DIVISION OF HAY HOUSE

Table of Contents

To my Children..*v*

Love Is My Constant Companion.. *vii*

Our Journey..*x*

Divine Love..*2*

My Vision..*3*

Source..*4*

Space..*5*

Stillness..*6*

The Wise One..*8*

Be Still..*8*

Encounter..*9*

Bliss...*10*

Beauty...*10*

Kim...*11*

Magic Moccasins..*12*

Softly...*12*

Free Spirit...*14*

Abundance...*15*

Letting Go...*16*

Observing..*17*

Prophecy..*18*

Separation..*18*

Peace...*19*

Timeless..*19*

Gentleness..*20*

Flame...*20*

The Observer..*21*

Purpose..*21*

The Unicorn *22*

Ears...*23*

Shadow *25*

A Gift Of Grace *27*

Grace...*28*

Mother Nature..*30*

To my Children

Debbie, Keith, Gary & Alison
My best pals always &
Beautiful blessings in my life.

Love Is My Constant Companion

Many years ago I started out on a journey to make sense of what was happening in my life. The reason I can write about this now is because I have succeeded in doing just that. Feeling as I do at this moment I can honestly say, it has all been worthwhile. It takes a lot of courage to keep digging away, so many times I felt like giving up, but I got the strength to continue.
Now I can look back and be very grateful for the help I had along the way. What prompted me to set out on this quest in the first place? Following an operation from which I was recovering very slowly and my subsequent visit to a healer, I became interested in natural healing and I started meditating. There was something very comforting when I succeeded in quieting my mind and I wanted more of this. I began to see more clearly that I was putting up with life. With circumstances that were very unsatisfactory. Now I could see so clearly that I had been accepting so little for myself for so long that it became a natural part of my life, but the real truth was that it was not natural to live like this anymore.
I decided to do something about it. I had to completely uproot every unhealthy thought I had about myself, so that I could see with new eyes. I had to be very disciplined and keep digging and uprooting. The ego can get very nervous when this happens, because it does not like change. It will do it's best to keep you stuck because when you're stuck it feels safe. So many times I have felt like I was being torn apart; this helps me to under-derstand and have compassion for people who do not want to deal with finding themselves. It is only by doing

this that you can really start living.

The peace I feel now is so beautiful and I can see now that love has always been my constant companion, but there were so many unhealthy beliefs I had about myself, that love was well and truly hidden. Now I see myself and everyone as innocent, even in the most painful and unhappy situations. The person I was with was mirroring what I needed to work on. The Intelligence within always arranges the perfect conditions, sends the perfect people into our life to help us grow. If we could understand this when we are going through a bad patch, we would see the circumstances as a blessing. I know sometimes we just want to run away and not face it, but it will only come up in different situations. So why not deal with it so the situation can heal.

The truth is, we have forgotten our birthright. But now that we can see the truth for what it is, we can step back and allow the Presence within to take over to show us the way. We can now surrender and allow life to find us. This means having total trust in the Presence, the one who has always been here for us, who we ignored because the voice of the ego became strong when we felt frightened. Now, however we have found out true voice, we can take time to savour every moment of our time together. This is the greatest gift we can give to ourselves, now we can be a gift to others.

There are many ways to remove the illusion of separation and meditation is a really good place to start. This because when we practice meditation, it becomes easier to still the mind and listen to that still voice within and with practice we can just be there with the breath, feeling the love of who we are. Being in nature is

*also a lovely way to come into the stillness. It takes
practice to live in this way, it also becomes easier the
more we practice and the benefits are wonderful.
I see myself living more and more from this place within
and I only have to breathe in to feel the love of who I
am. I feel this love as pure Essence flowing through me.
So what does Essence mean to me?
It is a feeling, it is who I am, it is the one looking out
through my eyes, the one animating my body. Listening
to beautiful music with me, dancing the dance of life
with me. The one who has been so patient when I lost my
way and so happy to welcome me when I found
my way home.
This could be likened to the parable of the prodigal son,
who went in search of whatever he thought would bring
him happiness. Only to return because he never did find
what he was searching for "out there", because it was
already inside of him.
We are the one we have been searching for and when
we come home to this truth we make room for the
Divine Presence to live life through us. Now we are
perfect partners, enjoying a mystical marriage with
Our Beloved. We are the Beloved.*

Our Journey

As children we know we are limitless, so what happens along the way? Life happens along the way. Circumstances that throw us off balance, until we forget who we really are. Many of us can go on for years thinking, this is ok, but sooner or later the child that had that beautiful dream of what life is all about wants to be heard. We wonder why we are beginning to feel unsettled. We start to question ourselves, am I happy as I am? Is there more to life than this? Most of us do not like change so we decide that this is alright, it feels safe. We, make ourselves busy so that we don't have time for unsettling thoughts. However now is the time to listen, and when we do we are guided to where we can get the answers. It may be a visit to the library where a book practically falls into our hands. It may be something someone says to us that strikes a chord. It could even be a wonderful idea that comes into our mind and once we really start to listen, we begin a journey to get to know ourselves all over again. This journey can be very unsettling at times and it takes a lot of courage to hang on in there. We always have help along the way as we are never alone. This journey leads us to within the very core of our being, where we uncover a treasure so precious, that nothing can knock us off balance. Then we can live our dreams and create magic in our life.

Soul Expressions

Highgate Park London 2004

Divine Love

*The call of the bird the call of the Divine; reminding us
to wake up to the beauty that is all around us.*

*Today Mother Nature is laying a carpet of golden
leaves at my feet. As the beautiful tree sheds her leaves.
Making room for new growth.*

*We too, let go of situations and conditions in our life
that no longer nourish us. Making way for new happenings,
new experiences to fill our life, open to the wonder
of it all.*

Highgate Park London 2004

My Vision

I stood beneath your branches as the wind was blowing strong
As I stood I felt your beautiful strength and became one with you as you stood firm.

You talked to me of my vision and were willing me to hold on.
You must have read my thoughts, because at times I
have felt like giving up, when it seemed I was getting no nearer.

It was lovely to hear you say "don't give up", from
where I'm standing it is beautiful and worth holding on to.

I felt your strength become my strength and I knew just
like you, I would stand firm and tall and all would be well.

Source

From the source of love we came on a journey of discovery, winding our way in and out of so many new experiences.

Learning and growing and moving on knowing that each step was bringing us closer to home.

Only to discover when we had finally made our way home, we had never been away.

Mall Ballyshannon Donegal 2012

Space

*I want to stay in this timeless space, where I can
experience a love as precious as this.*

*The past has been preparing me for where I am right
now.*

*I can now look on the past as a stepping stone,
a blessing in disguise, a gift indeed.*

Near Kells Gardens 2013

Stillness

In the stillness we know beyond a shadow of doubt, that all things are possible. Not only do we know they are possible, we know they are already taken care of.

God knows our goals and dreams before we do, as they are all God's promptings to express through us.

When we surrender to God's plan for us, life becomes effortless and so easy. All we have to do is stay open to his promptings.

He talks to us in so many wonderful ways, and life takes on a whole new meaning, when we take time to be still and listen.

Kells Gardens Waterfall 2013

The Wise One

*I surrender to the wise one, step into my magic
moccasins eager and happy to follow the guidance of
my companion on this adventure.*

*Our minds are one, a new day a new page to write in
my book of life.*

Be Still

*Be still listening to the silence, take time to reflect,
digest.*

*A time of preparation, allowing the beauty to shine
through.*

Beautiful colours expanding out into the universe.

*Preparing the way for the wonderful plan to unfold,
effortless, be still.*

Kells Gardens 2013

Encounter

Each and every encounter is a sacred encounter.
When we are present in the moment we are awake to
what is really taking place.

God is always talking to us and life takes on a whole
new meaning when we are present, to what is really
taking place.

Bliss

*The bliss of remembering who we really are brings
peace and contentment into our lives.*

*Everything takes on a new meaning. We are looking at
the world and everyone with new eyes, including
ourselves.*

*This helps us to be more understanding, more
compassionate and loving. There is nothing to forgive,
this is truly living our bliss.*

Beauty

*When we can see the beauty within everyone,
we have found the true beauty within ourselves.*

Kim

He asked for so little he gave so much, he loved me from the depths of his being.

He looked at me with eyes of love, talking to me with those beautiful eyes.

He came to me for a special reason. I missed him so much when he had to go.

But now he is back and our beautiful bond is stronger than ever. Both of us stronger, both of us wiser, sharing this wonderful journey together.

Magic Moccasins

*My magic moccasins beckoned me to a church not far
away.
I allowed my steps to guide me, and take me where they
may.*

*Inside I found a treasure as precious as can be, not
gold or silver, not wealth or fame, but a love that set
me free.*

Softly

*Speak softly of everyone, we are all brothers and
sisters learning and growing as best we can.*

*Speak softly of yourself, you too have always done
your best in all situations.*

*Think soft thoughts and let them sink deeply, so that
they soothe and nourish your mind.*

*Thoughts such as these are food for your soul, your
body, your entire being. The food of life.*

"Anna" My Silver Birch 2014

Free Spirit

The waiting is over, the little one has been set free to live life to the fullest. She can now sit back and allow herself to be taken care of.

She can be as carefree as can be enjoying her heart's desires, there are no limits.

She has crossed the threshold, there is no turning back, and why would she want to when she has all she needs here and now.

She is where miracles happen, creating whatever she desires. Absolutely limitless, and it just gets better and better.

So happy so content, a child of the universe, knowing it is her birthright to enjoy all the magic and wonders of this blissful adventure.

Abundance

*Abundance is having all the riches and treasures of the
universe. Seeing and experiencing them as a
beautiful flow of love to enjoy to the fullest, dancing
and weaving their way to me.*

*I can hear the music of abundance, I become one with
the flow. This is a natural happening for me because I
love music and dance, now I become one with
abundance. I am abundance.*

Sunset Ballyshannon Donegal 2012

Letting Go

In leaving the past behind life takes on a whole new meaning, no baggage to carry just beautiful new experiences.

We can put our energy into creating a beautiful future, while at the same time being content to live in the moment, seeing everyone as if for the first time.

Feeling light and carefree and at peace, this is a beautiful state to be in, our natural state.

Old Mill Sunset Ballyshannon Donegal 2012

Observing

Looking at a bird on the wall before it takes flight.
I can sense just how effortless it all is to him.
He already knows his destination.

He doesn't wonder how he will get there, his energy
has already gone ahead of him, while he is enjoying
where he is in this moment.

Observing everything around him ~~~ He is simply Being.

Today I take a lesson from this tiny bird, enjoying
where I am while knowing that my energy has
already gone ahead taking care of my hearts desires.

Seeing all of this as a reality in my life, this is true freedom.
Like that tiny bird I am just being. We are one and the same energy.

Near Muckross 2010

Prophecy

*It's all unfolding effortlessly, nothing can hold back
my vision now that it's time has come*

*I can feel this energy that I am in my vision, and my
vision in this energy.*

Separation

*I had to stand alone to know I was not alone, to
know there are no boundaries, no separations.*

*The only separation was in my mind and I am in
control of my mind.*

Old Mill Ballyshannon Donegal 2012

Peace

Your long hard struggle is over, I knew you would see it through

*You bent like the willow stood tall like the oak, and
walked with your head held high.*

*You have walked through the door marked struggle
no more, and now you may reach for the sky.*

Timeless

Timeless space less eternity, it is all taking place here and now.

Each moment perfect as it is: total surrender.

Kells Garden 2014

Gentleness

*I feel a beautiful gentleness in my thoughts, I feel it in
my breath.*

*It feels like the whisper of an angel, God's grace fills me
completely.*

Flame

*There is one flame one heartbeat. We have come
together in this body, moving together in perfect harmony.*

*Expressing love at all times. Life opens up and is now
a beautiful expression of our love.*

Kells Garden 2014

The Observer

Watching the world go by from this timeless space, being a part of it, yet apart from it.

In control, yet not controlling. Moving from one dimension and back in an instant.

Simplicity in itself, easy as a two year old, easy once again.

Purpose

The more I see and experience all that is happening in my life, the more humble I become.

There is perfection in everything; God's way is beautiful, everything has a purpose.

All we have to do is be patient, stay in the flow, trusting that it is all unfolding perfectly.

The Unicorn

*A magical being, the antenna at his crown is a
reminder that we all have access to a higher power. As
in the universal force constantly flowing in
through our crown chakra.*

*We are never cut off from this, as we are all one with
the universe. Our thoughts go out into the universe
and this is how our hopes and dreams are manifest
and so like the unicorn we are magical.*

Kells Garden 2014

Ears

There were times when my ears did not want to hear anymore, enough was enough. All I wanted was a good night's sleep snug in my bed. Only to hear those heavy footsteps overhead, to hear that mad laugh once again.

It seemed like there was no escape, nowhere to run. Until one day I made friends with the person who was the cause of my discomfort. Now the sounds in my ears did not seem so fierce, so frightening.

I could pretend I was listening to a happy person dancing lightly on the ceiling. I was relaxed, my ears relaxed, now I was listening in a way I was not able to before.

There was no more fear, there was understanding, and there was compassion. This was the beginning of a new way of dealing with everything in life, in always being able to hear and see a brighter side. A way out of the darkness.

Kells Garden 2014

Shadow

*Do not give the past and what has gone by a second
thought, the old stuff no longer has any substance.
Look to me, I am freedom in motion, step into my
shadow.*

*Now look behind, what you see is yourself and
everyone else learning and growing in the only way
you all knew how.*

*Gather the gifts you have picked up along the way and
put them to good use, there was a reason for every
happening.*

*You are ready to build on what you have learned, on
where you find yourself in this moment.*

*A whole new life is waiting to be lived, create bigger
and bolder dreams and see them come true for you.
Now step back, relax and enjoy.*

Kells Garden 2014

A Gift Of Grace

When Grace comes, it is so like drawing that last breath, the release from the earthly existence, except our physical body is still alive.

Much the same as when a new life is born, the little one is in a state of grace. Now life is taking place through you, life is effortless richer, so much more rewarding.
"A celebration."

Kells Garden 2014

Grace

To be in the state where we can allow grace to take over, live through us, is I feel what we have been striving for. What all the soul searching has been about. This is the gift we can embrace totally and completely.

Grace comes when we are ready, we can welcome grace like a long lost friend. Grace is our Beloved and we have no doubt we are loved, we are the Beloved.

Everything else falls away, there is always only this moment, where we are living our heaven on earth, our natural state. Now our life on earth is one huge celebration and this is the reason we are here, to celebrate life on earth.

The Mall Ballyshannon Donegal 2012

Mother Nature

These photos are reminders of the beauty that is everywhere. Some are from my time in London and Ballyshannon and more recently, my time in Kerry.

Living in London was busy but I always took time to visit the parks, to be quiet and sit by the many ponds in Highgate. There was something special about the trees there, they seemed to span out for miles.
When I moved to Ballyshannon in Donegal it didn't take me long to find so many peaceful places, such as sitting at the Mall Quay watching the fishermen enjoy the peace and quiet there. As for myself, I enjoyed the feeling of peace from the river as it flowed so gently, reminding me of the beauty of going with the flow, and allowing life to be.
I have found so many beautiful places here in Killarney, the river walk is something not to be missed and the peace and quiet beside the river is wonderful. Visiting Kells Gardens and the area all around is just a wonderland of colours.

I'm so happy I took the time to seek out all of these beautiful places, they have helped me find the peace within, and today I thank Mother Nature for all her beautiful gifts.

The Mall Ballyshannon Donegal 2012

Kells Garden 2014

Near Kells Garden 2014

Killarney National Park 2014

Printed in the United States
By Bookmasters